THE MANAGEMENT OF
INTERCULTURAL RELATIONS
IN
INTERNATIONAL BUSINESS

A Directory Of Resources

Editor
GEORGE W. RENWICK

•

Contributors
NANCY J. ADLER and ROBERT T. MORAN
GEORGE W. RENWICK and PAUL W. RUSSELL

Published by

INTERCULTURAL PRESS, INC.

70 WEST HUBBARD STREET
CHICAGO, ILLINOIS 60610

COPYRIGHT © 1982 BY INTERCULTURAL PRESS, INC.

Library of Congress Catalogue Card No. 81-85715
ISBN 0-933662-23-8

FIRST PRINTING
PRINTED IN THE UNITED STATES OF AMERICA

INTRODUCTION

Most of us who are responsible for overseas contacts, contracts and operations are continuously looking for reliable information about intercultural relations. We need such information because productive intercultural relations are increasingly important to our success (in fact, to our survival).

This Directory is the first attempt to pull together and make available what each of us has learned about intercultural relations over the years. The articles, reports and books included here have been selected because they can be of immediate use to personnel in organizations doing business overseas, and to faculty members and trainers conducting courses and programs on international management.

The experience and research of 238 authors are represented in this record of resources. Pertinent articles have been chosen from sixty-four journals.

Our common objective, of course, is to ensure that personnel in the coming years will have the special insights and skills necessary to perform confidently and effectively in demanding situations with men and women from diverse cultures. This kind of competence--intercultural competence--can be enhanced through the research and experiences represented here, and through carefully designed cross-cultural training programs based on it.

Included in the Directory are sources which describe and explain the <u>interaction</u> between people from contrasting cultural backgrounds--people whose assumptions and priorities are different, unexpected,

sometimes conflicting, and often unrecognized
barriers to business transactions. Not included are materials describing just one country
or comparing two countries. These can be found
elsewhere. Interesting to be sure, they usually
do not provide the practical explanations we need
when we are actually dealing with individuals and
organizations whose ways are not our ways. For
these, information on communication and interaction is essential.

The contributors have therefore located
information on the interaction involved whenever
organizations transfer personnel, families, ideas,
procedures, products or services from one dis-
tinctive culture into another.

All of the sources here are easily available in or through many public libraries, most
university libraries, and directly from the
publishing organizations themselves. Further
information on specific areas can be obtained
through writing particular authors in care of
their publishers. (Addresses for publishers
are available from any bookstore or by calling
the Reference Desk at a library.)

Because this is the first attempt at
gathering these resources, we have undoubtedly
missed some. We therefore apologize to the
authors of those resources not included and
will welcome suggestions for additions. As
these are received, and as new materials become
available, the Directory will be expanded and
printed again. Suggestions should be sent to
the Editor of the Directory at the Intercultural Press.

We hope those using the Directory will
find it helpful, and will contribute to making
it more so during the coming years.

George W. Renwick
November, 1981

CONTRIBUTORS

Nancy J. Adler

Dr. Adler is an Assistant Professor of Organizational Behavior and Cross-Cultural Management at McGill University in Montreal. She has been on the faculty of the American Graduate School of International Management in Glendale, Arizona and INSEAD in Fontainebleau, France. She serves as a management and cross-cultural consultant to multinational corporations based in Canada and the U.S.

Robert T. Moran

Dr. Moran is Director of the Program in Cross-Cultural Communication and Associate Professor of International Studies at the American Graduate School of International Management in Glendale, Arizona. Through Intercultural Communication, Inc., in Minneapolis, Minnesota, of which he is President, he provides consulting and training services to a variety of international organizations.

George W. Renwick

Mr. Renwick is a private consultant to international business firms in the areas of executive development, cross-cultural training and evaluation. He is a Visiting Professor at the American Graduate School of International Management in Glendale, Arizona, and Associate Editor of the Intercultural Press in Chicago, Illinois.

Paul W. Russell

Mr. Russell is Manager of Management Development for Frito-Lay, Inc. in Dallas, Texas where he works on human resource planning and organizational structure. Previously, he was Assessment and Development Associate with Development Dimensions International in Pittsburgh, Pennsylvania.

TABLE OF CONTENTS

Page

1
GENERAL SOURCES

CULTURAL SYNERGY: THE MANAGEMENT OF CROSS-CULTURAL
ORGANIZATIONS
1   Adler, N.J., Trends and Issues in O.D.: Current
    Theory and Practice, Burke, W.W. and Goodstein,
    L.D. (eds.), San Diego, CA: University
    Associates, 1980, pp. 163-184.

SOCIAL AND CULTURAL FACTORS IN MANAGEMENT
2   Brand, W., Management International Review,
    No. 3, 1966, pp. 149-150.

OVERSEAS MANAGEMENT
3   Brannen, T.R. and Hodgson, F.X., New York, NY:
    McGraw-Hill Book Co., 1965.

CULTURAL ISSUES WITHIN MULTINATIONAL ORGANIZATIONS
4   Proceedings, XVIth International Congress
    of Applied Psychology, Amsterdam: Swets and
    Zeitlinger, 1969, pp. 447-454.

MANAGEMENT DEVELOPMENT: THE INTERNATIONAL PERSPECTIVE
5   deBettingnies, H.D., Management Development and
    Training Handbook, Taylor and Lippi, H. (eds.)
    New York, NY: McGraw-Hill, 1975.

THE CULTURAL DIMENSIONS OF TOP EXECUTIVES' CAREERS
6 deBettingnies, H.D. and Evans, L., Culture
and Management, Weinshall, T.O. (ed.),
Middlesex, England: Penguin Books, Ltd., 1977.

CROSS-CULTURAL COMMUNICATION THROUGH THE ARTS
7 Dillon, C.D., Columbia Journal of World
Business, Fall 1971, pp. 31-39.

PROBLEMS IN CROSS-CULTURAL MANAGEMENT
8 DiStefano, J., Western Ontario School of Business
Administration, London, Canada, Fall, 1975.

MULTINATIONAL CORPORATIONS: HUMAN BEHAVIOR IN
INTERNATIONAL GROUPS
9 Ferrari, S., Management International Review,
Vol. XII, No. 6, 1972, pp. 31-35.

CULTURAL DETERMINISM AND MANAGEMENT BEHAVIOR
10 Graves, D., Organizational Dynamics, Autumn
1972, 14. pp.

MANAGERIAL THINKING, AN INTERNATIONAL STUDY
11 Haire, M., Ghiselli, E. and Porter, L.W.,
New York, NY: John Wiley & Sons, 1966.

MANAGING CULTURAL DIFFERENCES
12 Harris, P.R. and Moran, R.T., Houston, TX:
Gulf Publishing Co., 1979.

OVERSEAS OPERATIONS: THEIR PERSONNEL IMPLICATIONS
13 Hayden, S.J., Management Report.No. 80,
American Management Association, 1964,
pp. 339-352.

CULTURE'S CONSEQUENCES: INTERNATIONAL DIFFERENCES
IN WORK-RELATED VALUES
14 Hofstede, G., Beverly Hills, CA: Sage
Publications, 1980.

CULTURAL FACTORS
15 Hsu, F.L., Economic Development: Principles
and Patterns, Williamson, H.F. and Buttrick,
J.A. (eds.), Englewood Cliffs, NJ: Prentice
Hall, 1954, p. 318.

CULTURAL ANALYSIS IN OVERSEAS OPERATIONS
16 Lee, J.A., Harvard Business Review, Vol. 44,
No. 2, March-April 1966, pp. 106-114.

EAST-WEST MANAGEMENT DETENTE?
17 McFeely, W.M., Conference Board Record,
August 1971, pp. 24-28.

THE GUIDEBOOK FOR INTERNATIONAL TRAINERS IN BUSINESS
AND INDUSTRY
18 Miller, V.A., New York, NY: Van Nostrand
Reinhold, 1979.

MANAGING CULTURAL SYNERGY
19 Moran, R.T. and Harris, P.R., Houston, TX:
Gulf Publishing Co., 1981.

MULTINATIONAL PEOPLE MANAGEMENT - A GUIDE FOR
ORGANIZATIONS AND EMPLOYEES
20 Noer, D.S., Washington, DC: The Bureau of
National Affairs, Inc., 1975.

EAST-WEST INTERNATIONAL INTERFIRM COOPERATION
21 Simai, M., The Conference Board Record,
October 1974, pp. 29-33.

THE MULTINATIONAL CORPORATION: MANAGEMENT MYTHS
22 Sirota, D., Personnel, January-February
1972, pp. 34-41.

MANAGEMENT AT HOME AND ABROAD
23 Spaght, M.E., Michigan Business Review,
November 1965, pp. 20-24.

4

THE CULTURAL ENVIRONMENT OF INTERNATIONAL BUSINESS
24 Terpstra, V., Cincinnati, OH: South-West
Publishing, 1978.

2
INTERCULTURAL COMMUNICATION IN BUSINESS

CROSS-NATIONAL MANAGERIAL INTERACTION: A CONCEPTUAL MODEL
25   DeLaTorre, J. and Toyne, B., <u>Academy of Management Review</u>, Vol. 3, No. 3, July 1978, pp. 462-475

THE SILENT LANGUAGE IN OVERSEAS BUSINESS
26   Hall, E.T., <u>Harvard Business Review</u>, May-June 1960.

INTERCULTURAL COMMUNICATION: A GUIDE TO MEN OF ACTION
27   Hall, E.T. and Whyte, W.F., <u>Human Organization</u>, Vol. 19, No. 1, Spring 1960, pp. 5-12.

THE INTERNATIONAL LANGUAGE OF MANAGEMENT
28   Hayes, J.L., <u>S.A.M. Advanced Management Journal</u>, Vol. 28, No. 4, October 1973, pp. 17-19.

COMMUNICATION BARRIERS BETWEEN GERMAN SUBSIDIARIES AND PARENT AMERICAN COMPANIES
29   Hildebrandt, H.W., <u>Michigan Business Review</u>, July 1973.

THE LANGUAGE OF INTERNATIONAL BUSINESS
30   <u>International Management</u>, May 1965.

6

BRIDGING CULTURAL BARRIERS IN INTERNATIONAL
MANAGEMENT
31   Stone, D.D., <u>S.A.M. Advanced Management Journal</u>,
January 1969, pp. 56-62.

INTERPERSONAL RELATIONS IN INTERNATIONAL ORGANIZATIONS
32   Triandis, H.C., Organizational Behavior and Human
Performance, Vol. 2, 1967, pp. 26-55.

3
NEGOTIATIONS (INTERNATIONAL)

PLANNING FOR INTERNATIONAL BUSINESS NEGOTIATIONS

33 Kapoor, A., Cambridge, MA: Ballinger
Publishing Company, 1975.

NEGOTIATING WITH THIRD WORLD GOVERNMENTS

34 Wells, L.T., Jr., Harvard Business Review,
January-February 1977, pp. 72-81.

4
MULTICULTURAL ORGANIZATIONAL DESIGN

STRUCTURAL SOURCES OF PERSONNEL PROBLEMS IN
MULTINATIONAL CORPORATIONS

35 Zeira, Y., Omega, Vol. 5, No. 2, April 1977,
pp. 161–172.

5
AMERICAN CULTURAL ASSUMPTIONS

CULTURAL ASSUMPTIONS UNDERLYING U.S. MANAGEMENT
CONCEPTS

36 Newman, W.H., <u>Management in an International
Context</u>, Massie, J.L. and Laytjies, J. (eds.),
New York, NY: Harper and Row, 1972.

<u>AMERICAN CULTURAL PATTERNS: A CROSS-CULTURAL
PERSPECTIVE</u>

37 Stewart, E.C., Chicago, IL: Intercultural
Press, Inc., 1979.

THE INTERNATIONAL EXECUTIVE'S BAGGAGE: CULTURAL
VALUES OF THE AMERICAN FRONTIER

38 Wallin, T.O., <u>M.S.U. Business Topics</u>, Spring
1976, pp. 49-58.

6

TRANSFER OF PERSONNEL

A. Selection

THE ASSIGNMENT OF AMERICAN EXECUTIVES ABROAD:
SYSTEMATIC, HAPHAZARD OR CHAOTIC?
39 Baker, J.C. and Ivancevich, J.M., <u>California
<u>Management Review</u>, Vol. XIII, No. 3, 1971,
pp. 39-44.

SELECTING MANAGERS: A STUDY OF THE PERSONNEL
SELECTION DECISION PROCESS
40 Bassett, G.A., Crontonville, NY: General
Electric Co., 1968.

SELECTING PERSONNEL FOR FOREIGN ASSIGNMENTS
41 Baum, C., Masters Thesis, Pepperdine Univer-
ity, 1976.

SELECTING AND TRAINING INTERNATIONAL MANAGERS
42 <u>Business International Research Report</u>,
Business International Corporation, New York,
NY: 1974.

EXPATRIATE SELECTION: INSURING SUCCESS AND
AVOIDING FAILURE
43 Hays, R.D., <u>Journal of International Business
<u>Studies</u>, Spring 1974.

WHAT BUSINESS CAN LEARN FROM PEACE CORPS SELECTION
AND TRAINING
44   Henry, E.R., Personnel, July-August 1965,
        pp. 17-26.

THE SELECTION OF OVERSEAS MANAGEMENT
45   Hodgson, F.X., M.S.U. Business Topics, Spring
        1963, pp. 49-54.

MODEL FOR THE DESIGN OF A SELECTION PROGRAM FOR
MULTINATIONAL EXECUTIVES
46   Howard, C.G., Public Personnel Management,
        March-April 1974, pp. 138-145.

SELECTION OF AMERICAN MANAGERS FOR OVERSEAS ASSIGNMENTS
47   Ivancevich, J.M., Personnel Journal, 1969,
        pp. 190-193.

AMERICANS SELECTED FOR OVERSEAS OPERATIONS
48   Loubert, J.D., McLean, VA: The Trans-Cultural
        Research and Training Institute (Contract
        NONR-4346-(00), NR-144-238), 1967.

PROBLEMS AND TRENDS IN ASSIGNING MANAGERS OVERSEAS
49   Maddox, R.C., Personnel, January-February 1971,
        pp. 53-56.

SELECTING AMERICANS FOR OVERSEAS ASSIGNMENTS
50   Mandell, M.M., Personnel Administrator, 1958,
        pp. 25-30.

SELECTING AMERICANS FOR OVERSEAS EMPLOYMENT
51   Mandell, M.M. and Greenberg, S.H., Personnel,
        March 1954, pp. 356-366.

THE INTERNATIONAL SELECTION DECISION: A STUDY OF SOME
DIMENSIONS OF MANAGERIAL BEHAVIOR IN THE SELECTION
PROCESS
52   Miller, E.L., Academy of Management Journal,
        Vol. 16, No. 2, June 1973, pp. 239-252.

THE OVERSEAS ASSIGNMENT: HOW MANAGERS DETERMINE WHO
IS SELECTED
53 Miller, E.L., Michigan Business Review, May
1972, pp. 12-19.

THE SELECTION DECISION FOR AN INTERNATIONAL ASSIGNMENT:
A STUDY OF THE DECISION MAKER'S BEHAVIOR
54 Miller, E.L., Journal of International Business
Studies, Fall, 1972, pp. 49-65.

MITSUI'S BIG MACHINE FOR CHOOSING, GROOMING ITS
INTERNATIONAL MANAGERS
55 Business International, July 18, 1975, pp. 228-
229.

THE DEVELOPMENT OF AN ATTITUDE MEASURING DEVICE FOR
IMPROVMENT OF SELECTION/SCREENING OF U.S. PERSONNEL
FOR OVERSEAS DUTY
56 Mozingo, T.P., Master's Thesis, Monterey, CA:
Naval Postgraduate School, December, 1974.

STEPS TO BETTER SELECTION AND TRAINING FOR OVERSEAS
JOBS
57 Peter, H.W. and Henry, E.R., Personnel,
January-February, 1962.

RECRUITING, SELECTING AND DEVELOPING PERSONNEL FOR
FOREIGN OPERATIONS
58 Management Record, December 1959.

SELECTING FOREIGN EXECUTIVES - ABI CHECKLIST
59 Business International, November 12, 1965,
pp. 366.

SELECTION, TRAINING, AND COMPENSATION OF OVERSEAS
MANAGERS
60 Business International, New York, 1958.

SELECTION OF OVERSEAS PERSONNEL
61 Stern, A.H., Personnel Journal, Vol. 45, No. 4,
1966, pp. 224.

SELECTING AND ORIENTING STAFF FOR SERVICE OVERSEAS
62   Teague, B.W., New York, NY: The Conference
Board, Inc., 1976

INTERNATIONAL MANAGEMENT SELECTION AND DEVELOPMENT
63   Teague, F.A., California Management Review,
Vol. XII, No. 3, Spring 1970, pp. 1-6.

THE SELECTION OF PERSONNEL FOR INTERNATIONAL SERVICE
64   Torre, M., World Federation for Mental Health,
Geneva, Switzerland, 1963.

SCREENING AND SELECTION FOR OVERSEAS ASSIGNMENTS:
ASSESSMENT AND RECOMMENDATIONS TO THE U.S. NAVY
65   Tucker, M.F., Denver, CO: Center for Research
and Education, 1974.

OVERVIEW SUMMARY FOR AN ASSESSMENT OF THE SCREENING
PROBLEM FOR OVERSEAS ASSIGNMENT
66   Tucker, M.F. and Schiller, J.E., Denver, CO:
Center for Research and Education, May 1975.

RECRUITMENT AND SELECTION FOR WORK IN FOREIGN
CULTURES
67   Wilson, A.T.M., Human Relations, Vol. 14,
No. 1, 1961, pp. 3-21.

SELECTION OF PERSONNEL FOR OVERSEAS EMPLOYMENT - A
REVIEW OF THE LITERATURE
68   Woodruff, E., Personnel Administrator, Vol. 15,
No. 4, July 1952, pp. 20-24.

THE PERSONNEL ASSESSMENT CENTER: AN AID IN THE
SELECTION OF PERSONNEL FOR CROSS-CULTURAL ASSIGNMENTS
69   Zuga, F.L., Monterey, CA: Naval Post-Graduate
School, March 1975.

B. Preparation for
Overseas Assignments

1. Materials

RELOCATION GUIDE
70   Brasch, R., South Field, MO: Executive Publications, Ltd.

AMERICAN MANAGEMENT ABROAD: A HANDBOOK FOR THE BUSINESS EXECUTIVE OVERSEAS
71   Bryson, G.D., New York, NY: Harper & Brothers, 1961.

DIRECTORY OF INTERNATIONAL BUSINESS TRAVEL AND RELOCATION
72   Detroit, MI: Gale Research Co., Book Tower Building, 1980.

SURVIVAL KIT FOR OVERSEAS LIVING
73   Kohls, L.R., Chicago, IL: Intercultural Press, Inc., 1979.

UPDATES
74 Lanier, A.R., Chicago, IL: Intercultural Press, Inc., Volumes now available on the following countries:

Bahrain/Qatar	Kuwait
Belgium	Mexico
Brazil	Nigeria
Britain	Saudi Arabia
Egypt	Singapore
France	South Korea
Hong Kong	R.O.C. (Taiwan)
Indonesia	Venezuela
Japan	West Germany
	United Arab Emirates

YOUR MANAGER ABROAD: HOW WELCOME? HOW PREPARED?
75 Lanier, A.R., AMA Management Briefings, New York, NY: American Management Association, 1975.

SO YOU'RE GOING ABROAD...ARE YOU PREPARED?
76 Moran, R.T., Minneapolis, MN: Intercultural Communication, Inc. (P.O. Box 14358, Minneapolis, MN, 55414), 1980, 18 pp.

PREPARATION FOR ASSIGNMENT ABROAD - A CHECKLIST ON WHAT TO TAKE - AND WHAT TO EXPECT
77 Business International, May 29, 1970, pp. 172-173.

EVALUATION HANDBOOK FOR CROSS-CULTURAL TRAINING
78 Renwick, G.W., Chicago, IL: Intercultural Press, 1978.

INTERACTS: INTERCULTURAL RELATIONS IN BUSINESS
79 Renwick, G.W., (ed.), Chicago, IL: Intercultural Press, Inc. Volumes now available or in preparation are:

Australia - U.S., Renwick, G.W.
Mexico - U.S., Condon, J.C.
Thailand - U.S., Fieg, J.P.
French and English in Canada, Hawes, F.
Japan - U.S., Condon, J.C.
Malaysia - U.S., Renwick, G.W.

QUESTIONNAIRE ON CROSS-CULTURAL MANAGEMENT PERSPECTIVES
80 Rhinesmith, S.H. and Renwick, G.W., Managing Cultural Differences, Harris, P.R. and Moran, R.T., Houston, TX: Gulf Publishing Co., 1979, pp. 370-376.

B. Preparation for Overseas Assignments

2. Training

SKILL TRAINING FOR FOREIGN ASSIGNMENT: THE RELUCTANT
U.S. CASE

81   Ackermann, J.M., <u>Intercultural Communication</u>:
<u>A Reader</u>, Samovar, L.A. and Porter, R.E.,
Second Edition, Belmont, CA: Wadsworth
Publishing Co., 1976.

HOW FIRMS PREPARE EXECUTIVES FOR FOREIGN POSTS

82   <u>Business International</u>, August 14, 1970, p. 262

MITSUI'S BIG MACHINE FOR CHOOSING, GROOMING ITS
INTERNATIONAL MANAGERS

83   <u>Business International</u>, July 18, 1975,
pp. 228-229.

SELECTING AND TRAINING INTERNATIONAL MANAGERS

84   <u>Business International Research Report</u>, New
York, NY: Business International Corporation,
1974.

SELECTION, TRAINING, AND COMPENSATION OF OVERSEAS
MANAGERS

85   New York, NY: <u>Business International</u>, 1958.

DEVELOPING THE INTERNATIONAL EXECUTIVE

86   Chorafas, D.N., <u>AMA Research Study #83</u>,
American Management Association, 1967.

ART OF OVERSEASMANSHIP: PREPARING AMERICANS FOR WORK
ABROAD IN BUSINESS, INDUSTRY, AND GOVERNMENT
87 Cleveland, H. and Mangone, G.J. (eds.), Public
    Administration Review, 1958, pp. 136-139.

NEW PERSPECTIVES IN TRAINING AND ASSESSMENT OF OVER-
SEAS PERSONNEL
88 Daniel, J. and Stewart, E.C., Human Resources
    Research Office Professional Paper, Alexandria,
    VA: George Washington University, February 1967,
    15 pp.

CASE METHODS IN INTERNATIONAL MANAGEMENT TRAINING
89 DiStefano, J.J., Handbook of International
    Communication, Asante, M.K., Newmark, E., and
    Blake, C.A., Beverly Hills, CA: Sage Publica-
    tions, 1979.

MORE EFFECTIVE TRAINING FOR OVERSEAS MANAGEMENT
THROUGH PROJECTIVE TECHNIQUES
90 Ewing, J.S., Boston University Business Review,
    Winter 1963-1964, pp. 21-30.

A JOURNEY FOR WORLD PERSPECTIVE: DEVELOPMENT
EXPERIENCE FOR THE MULTI-NATIONAL MANAGER
91 Fleming, J.E., Training and Development Journal,
    June 1973.

TRAINING EXPATRIATES FOR MANAGERIAL ASSIGNMENT IN
JAPAN
92 Harrari, E. and Zeira, Y., California
    Management Review, Vol. 20, No. 4, Summer 1978,
    pp. 56-62.

INTERCULTURAL EDUCATION FOR MULTI-NATIONAL MANAGERS
93 Harris, P.R. and Harris, D.L., International
    and Intercultural Communication Annual, Speech
    Communication Association, Vol. 3, December
    1976, pp. 70-85.

ORGANIZATIONAL RESPONSIBILITIES AND CULTURAL
DIFFERENCES
94 Harris, P.R. and Moran, R.T., Managing
Cultural Differences; Unit 3, Houston, TX:
Gulf Publishing Co., 1979, pp. 82-100.

PREPARING MANAGERS FOR INTERNATIONAL OPERATIONS
95 Hawrylyshyn, B., Business Quarterly, 1967.

DEVELOPING OVERSEAS MANAGERS AND MANAGERS OVERSEAS
96 Illman, P.E., New York, NY: AMACOM, 1979.

PREDEPARTURE TRAINING FOR OVERSEAS
97 Ivancevich, J.M., Training and Development
Journal, February 1969.

TRAINING NEEDS OF AMERICANS WORKING ABROAD
98 Johnson, M.B. and Carter, G.L. Jr., Social
Change, 1972, pp. 1-3.

TRAINING EMPLOYEES FOR SERVICE ABROAD: THE NEED FOR
UNDERSTANDING HUMAN INTERACTION-A SUGGESTED USE FOR
SENSITIVITY
99 Mills, R.C., Training Directors Journal,
January 1964, pp. 12-18.

ORIENTATION TO ANOTHER SOCIETY: TRAINING FOR
INTERCULTURAL EFFECTIVENESS
100 Nath, R., Kultura, Vol. 17, 1972, pp. 155-170.

TRAINING INTERNATIONAL BUSINESS AND MANAGEMENT
PERSONNEL: A CONTINGENCY APPROACH
101 Nath, R., Overview of Intercultural Education,
Training and Research, Vol. II, Hoopes, D.S.,
Pedersen, P.B. and Renwick G.W. (eds.),
Chicago, IL: Intercultural Press, Inc., 1978,
pp. 135-147.

TRAINING PROGRAMS TO PREPARE EXECUTIVES FOR INTER-
NATIONAL BUSINESS AND MORE PARTICULARLY FOR CROSS-
CULTURAL MANAGEMENT ASSIGNMENTS

102 Pedraglio, G., Comparative Management:
Teaching, Training and Research, New York
University, Graduate School of Business
Administration, 1970.

STEPS TO BETTER SELECTION AND TRAINING FOR OVERSEAS
JOBS

103 Peter, H.W. and Henry, E.R., Personnel,
January-February 1962.

RECRUITING, SELECTING AND DEVELOPING PERSONNEL FOR
FOREIGN OPERATIONS

104 Management Record, December 1959.

MULTINATIONAL TRAINING FOR MULTINATIONAL CORPORATIONS

105 Schnapper, M., Handbook of Intercultural
Communication, Asante, M.K., Newmark, E. and
Blake, C.A., Beverly Hills, CA: Sage Publica-
tions, 1979.

CROSS-CULTURAL ORIENTATION FOR OVERSEAS EMPLOYEES

106 Shabaz, W.O., The Personnel Administrator,
May 1978.

THEY LEARN THE LOCAL RULES BEFORE WORKING ABROAD

107 Spaght, M.E., International Commerce, March 6,
1967, pp. 4-5.

SELECTING AND ORIENTING STAFF FOR SERVICE OVERSEAS

108 Teague, B.W., New York, NY: The Conference
Board, Inc., 1976.

INTERNATIONAL MANAGEMENT SELECTION AND DEVELOPMENT

109 Teague, F.A., California Management Review,
Vol. XII, No. 3, Spring 1970, pp. 1-6.

CROSS-CULTURAL TRAINING FOR OVERSEAS MANAGEMENT

110 Thiagarajan, K.M., Management International
Review, Vols. 4-5, 1971, pp. 69-85.

IMPROVING CROSS-CULTURAL TRAINING AND MEASUREMENT OF
CROSS-CULTURAL LEARNING
111 Tucker, M., Raik, H., Rossitor, D. and Uhes, M.,
     Denver, CO: Center for Research and Education,
     1973.

BUSINESSMEN ARE BEING TRAINED TO BE NOT SO INNOCENT
ABROAD
112 Wilke, G., The New York Times, January 30, 1966.

TRAINING OF EXPATRIATES FOR MANAGERIAL ASSIGNMENTS
IN JAPAN
113 Zeira, Y. and Harari, E., California Management
     Review, Vol. 20, No. 4, Summer 1978.

C. American Personnel Overseas: Qualities, Roles, Performance

AWARENESS LEVELS OF EMPLOYEES CONSIDERING OVERSEAS
RELOCATION
114a Acuff, F.L., Personnel Journal, November 1974,
pp. 809-812.

WOMEN AS ANDROGYNOUS MANAGERS: A CONCEPTUALIZATION OF
THE POTENTIAL FOR AMERICAN WOMEN IN INTERNATIONAL
MANAGEMENT
114b Adler, N.J., International Journal of Intercultural Relations, Vol. 3, No. 4, 1979, pp. 407-436

THE MULTINATIONAL MAN-THE ROLE OF THE MANAGER ABROAD
115 Aitken, T., London: George Allen & Unwin Ltd.,
1973

INTERCULTURAL COMMUNICATION AND THE MNC EXECUTIVE
116 Almaney, A., Columbia Journal of World Business,
Winter 1974.

DRIFT TO AUTHORITARIANISM: THE CHANGING MANAGERIAL
STYLES OF THE U.S. EXECTUVIE OVERSEAS
117 Alpander, G.G., Journal of International
Business Studies, Vol. 4, Fall 1974, pp. -113.

AMERICANS ABROAD
118 Annals of the American Academy of Political and
Social Science, 1966, pp. 1-170.

THE AMERICAN ADVISOR ABROAD
119 Bass, B.M., Journal of Applied Behavioural
Science, Vol. 7, No. 3, May-June 1971, pp. 285-
307.

MANAGERS ABROAD--THEY'RE DIFFERENT

120 Benge, E.J. SAM Advanced Management Journal, April 1968.

THE NEW NOMADS

121 Bravlove, M., Wall Street Journal, August 1, 1973.

ASSIGNMENT TO AMBIGUITY: WORK PERFORMANCE IN CROSS-CULTURAL TECHNICAL ASSISTANCE

122 Byrnes, F.C., Human Organization, 1964, pp. 196-209.

THE AMERICAN OVERSEAS

123 Cangemi, J.P., Personnel Journal, 1969, pp. 118-120.

THE CHANGING ROLE OF THE INTERNATIONAL EXECUTIVE

124 New York, NY: National Industrial Conference Board, 1966.

THE OVERSEAS AMERICANS

125 Cleveland, H., Mangone, G.J. and Adams, J.C., New York, NY: McGraw-Hill Book Co., 1960.

THE EXECUTIVE OVERSEAS: ADMINISTRATIVE ATTITUDES AND RELATIONSHIPS IN A FOREIGN CULTURE

126 Fayerweather, J., Syracuse, NY: Syracuse University Press, 1959.

THE U.S. OVERSEAS EXECUTIVE: HIS ORIENTATION AND CAREER PATTERNS

127 Gonzales, R.F. and Neghandi, A.R., East Lansing, MI: MSU Graduate School of Business Administration, 1967.

TOMORROW'S EXECUTIVE: A MAN FOR ALL COUNTRIES

128 Haider, M.L., Columbia Journal of World Business, Vol. 1, No. 1, Winter 1966, pp. 107-113.

24

PEOPLE PROBLEMS ABROAD
129 Hall, R.D., Business Abroad, September 20, 1965, pp. 17-19.

PERSONNEL PROBLEMS IN OVERSEAS OPERATIONS
130 Hayden, S., Personnel, May-June 1968, pp. 14-28.

ASCRIBED BEHAVIORAL DETERMINANTS OF SUCCESS-FAILURE
AMONG U.S. EXPATRIATE MANAGERS
131 Hays, R.D., Journal of International Business Studies, Spring 1971, Vol. 2, No. 1, pp. 40-46.

THE CORPORATE EXPATRIATE: ASSIGNMENT TO AMBIGUITY
132 Heenan, D.A., Columbia Journal of World Business, May-June 1970, pp. 49-54.

WHY EXECUTIVES FAIL ABROAD
133 Howard, C.G., Human Resource Management, Vol. II, No. 1, Spring 1972, pp. 32-36.

PERCEIVED NEED SATISFACTION OF DOMESTIC VERSUS
OVERSEAS MANAGERS
134 Ivancevich, J.M., Journal of Applied Psychology, Vol. 52, 1968, pp. 274-278.

A COMPARATIVE STUDY OF THE SATISFACTION OF DOMESTIC
UNITED STATES MANAGERS AND OVERSEAS UNITED STATES
MANAGERS
135 Ivancevich, J.M. and Baker, J.C., Academy of Management Journal, March 1970, pp. 69-77.

THE JOB SATISFACTION OF AMERICAN MANAGERS OVERSEAS
136 Ivancevich, J.M. and Baker, J.C., MSU Business Topics, Summer 1969, pp. 72-78.

WHAT IT TAKES TO BE A SUCCESSFUL INTERNATIONAL MANAGER
137 Kiernan, P., International Executive, Fall 1963, p. 3.

YOUR MANAGAGER ABROAD: HOW WELCOME? HOW PREPARED?
138 Lanier, A.R., AMA Management Briefings, New
York, NY: American Management Association, 1975

THE CHANGING ROLE OF THE INTERNATIONAL EXECUTIVES,
STUDIES IN BUSINESS POLICY
139 Lovell, E.B., No. 119 National Industrial
Conference Board, No. 119, 1966, 254 pp.

THE MANAGER OF THE FUTURE
140 McFeely, W.M., Columbia Journal of World
Business, May-June 1969, pp. 87-90.

THE INTERRELATIONSHIP AND INTERACTION BETWEEN THE
CULTURAL ENVIRONMENT AND MANAGERIAL EFFECTIVENESS
141 Megginson, L.C., Management International
Review, Vol. VII, No. 6, 1967, pp. 65-70.

MANAGERIAL QUALIFICATIONS OF PERSONNEL OCCUPYING
OVERSEAS MANAGEMENT POSITIONS AS PERCEIVED BY
AMERICAN EXPATRIATE MANAGERS
142 Miller, E.L., Journal of International Business
Studies, Spring-Summer 1977, pp. 57-68.

A STUDY OF EXPATRIATE AMERICAN MANAGERS' PERCEPTIONS
OF MANAGERIAL TRAITS AND CAPABILITIES OF THEIR
SUBORDINATES AND SUPERIORS
143 Miller, E.L., Academy of Management Proceedings, 1975, pp. 294-297.

ATTITUDES OF AMERICAN AND GERMAN EXPATRIATE MANAGERS
IN EUROPE AND LATIN AMERICA
144 Miller, E., Bhatt, B., Hill, R. and Catteaneo,
J., Academy of Management Proceedings, Vol. 40,
1980, pp. 53-57.

WHAT IT TAKES TO WORK ABROAD
145 Oates, D., International Management, October
1970.

MANAGERIAL VALUE PROFILES AS PREDICTORS OF POLICY
DECISIONS IN A CROSS-CULTURAL SETTING
146 Palmer, D.D., Veiga, J.F. and Vora, J.A.,
Academy of Management Proceedings, 1979, pp.
293-298.

EXECUTIVE TROUBLE ABROAD
147 Parks, F.N., Dun's Review, August 1963, pp. 35-
36, 70, 72.

HOW MULTINATIONAL SHOULD YOUR TOP MANAGERS BE?
148 Perlmutter, H.V. and Heenan, D.A., Harvard
Business Review, Vol. 52, No. 6, 1974, pp.
121-132.

INTER-CULTURAL COMPETENCE AND THE AMERICAN
BUSINESSMAN
149 Priceman, M., Training Directors Journal,
Vol. 19, No. 3, March 1965.

INTERNATIONAL JOBS AND CAREERS
150 Purcer-Smith, G., Industrial and Organizational
Psychology, Vol. 2, No. 2, Spring 1971, pp.
195-196.

THE NEW MULTINATIONAL MANAGERS
151 Reddig, W.M. Jr., Saturday Review, November
1969, pp. 35-41.

INTERNATIONAL MANAGER: A ROLE PROFILE
152 Shetty, Y.R., Management International Review,
1971, pp. 19-25.

EFFECTIVE PERFORMANCE OVERSEAS
153 Steiglitz, H., Management Record, February
1963.

FACTORS ASSOCIATED WITH EFFECTIVE PERFORMANCE IN
OVERSEAS WORK ASSIGNMENTS
154 Stoner, J.A., Aram, J.D. and Rubin, I.M.,
Personnel Psychology, Vol. 25, 1972, pp. 303-
319.

MYTHS THAT MISLEAD U.S. MANAGERS IN JAPAN
155 Tsurumi, Y., Harvard Business Review, July-
     August 1971, pp. 118-128.

EXPATRIATE EXECUTIVES: OVERPAID BUT UNDERCOMPENSATED
156 Vivian, J., Columbia Journal of World Business,
     January-February 1968, pp. 29-41.

ROLE CONFLICTS OF EXPATRIATE MANAGERS: A CONSTRUCT
157 Yun, C.K., Management International Review,
     Vol. 13, No. 6, 1973.

ROTATIONS OF EXPATRIATES IN MNC's
158 Zeira, Y., Management International Review,
     Vol. 16, No. 3, August 1976, pp. 37-46.

D. *Cultural Adjustment*

ROLE SHOCK: AN OCCUPATIONAL HAZARD OF AMERICAN
TECHNICAL ASSISTANTS ABROAD
   159   Byrnes, F.C., The Annals of the American
           Academy of Political and Social Science, 1966,
           pp. 95-108.

MANAGING CULTURAL SHOCK
   160   Harris, P.R. and Moran, R.T., Managing
           Cultural Differences; Chapter 7, Houston, TX:
           Gulf Publishing Co., 1979, pp. 82-100.

CROSS-CULTURAL STRESS AND ADAPTATION IN GLOBAL
ORGANIZATIONS
   161   Harvey, D.F., Case Western Reserve
           University, Volume 31/05-B, Dissertation
           Abstracts International, 2958, 1969.

THE EXECUTIVE ABROAD: MINIMIZING BEHAVIORAL PROBLEMS
   162   Hays, R.D., Business Horizons, June 1972,
           pp. 87-93.

THE TRAUMA OF THE TRANSFERRED EXECUTIVE
   163   Murray, T., Duns' Review, May 1971, pp. 40-43.

COMPARATIVE MANAGEMENT: A RESOURCE FOR IMPROVING
MANAGERIAL ADAPTABILITY
164   Newman, W.H., <u>Columbia Journal of World
Business,</u> Winter 1978, p. 5.

WHEN IN ROME, DO AS THE ROMANS DO?
165   Simonetti, J. and Simonetti, F., <u>Management
International Review,</u> Vol. 18, No. 3, 1978,
pp. 69-74.

INCIDENTS OF CULTURE SHOCK AMONG AMERICAN BUSINESSMEN
OVERSEAS
166   Stessin, L., <u>Pittsburgh Business Review,</u>
November-December 1971.

EXTRA PAY FOR EXECUTIVE CULTURE SHOCK
167   Teague, B.W., <u>The Conference Board Record,</u>
January 1975, pp. 18-21.

A RUGGED ROAD FOR EXECUTIVES WHO CONSTANTLY GET
MOVED
168   Tiger, L., <u>Los Angeles Times,</u> Sunday,
September 22, 1974, Part VI, p. 1+.

HOW TO EASE THE CULTURE SHOCK
169   Wilce, H., <u>International Management,</u> June 1971,
pp. 18-22.

E. Families Overseas

COPING WITH THE STRESSES OF TRAVEL AS AN OPPORTUNITY
FOR IMPROVING THE QUALITY OF WORK AND FAMILY LIFE
170 Culbert, S.A. and Renshaw, J.R., Family
Process, Vol 11, No. 3., September 1972,
pp. 321-337.

THE GAIJIN EXECUTIVE'S WIFE
171 Priestoff, N., The Conference Board Record,
Vol. XIII, No. 5, May 1976, pp. 51-64.

AN EXPLORATION OF THE DYNAMICS OF THE OVERLAPPING
WORLDS OF WORK AND FAMILY
172 Renshaw, J.R., Family Process, Vol. 15, No. 1,
March 1976, pp. 143-164.

CORPORATE WIVES - CORPORATE CASUALTIES
173 Seidenberg, R., New York, NY: AMACOM, 1973.

HAZARDS OF REARING CHILDREN IN FOREIGN COUNTRIES
174 Werkman, S.L., American Journal of Psychiatry,
Vol. 128, No. 8, February 1972, pp. 106-111

OVER HERE AND BACK THERE: AMERICAN ADOLESCENTS
OVERSEAS
175 Werkman, S.L., Foreign Service Journal, March
1975, pp. 13-16.

F. Re-entry

RE-ENTRY: MANAGING CROSS-CULTURAL TRANSITIONS
176 Adler, N.J., Group and Organization Studies, Vol. 6, No. 3, September 1981, pp. 341-356.

APPLYING NEW KNOWLEDGE IN THE BACK-HOME SETTING: A STUDY OF INDIAN MANAGERS' ADOPTIVE EFFORTS
177 Baumgartel, H. and Jeanpierre, F., Journal of Applied Behavioural Science, Vol. 8, No. 6, November-December 1972, pp. 674-695.

EXECUTIVE RE-ENTRY: PROBLEMS OF REPATRIATION
178 Cagney, B., Personnel Journal, September 1975.

EXECUTIVES FACE TROUBLE RETURNING FROM ABROAD
179 Wall Street Journal, August 18, 1975.

THE RETURNING OVERSEAS EXECUTIVE: CULTURAL SHOCK IN REVERSE
180 Howard, C.G., Human Resource Management, Summer 1974, pp. 22-26.

INTERNATIONAL PERSONNEL REPATRIATION: CULTURAL SHOCK IN REVERSE
181 Murray, J.A., M.S.U. Business Topics, Vol. 21, No. 2, Summer 1973, pp. 59-66.

INTEGRATING FOREIGN SERVICE EMPLOYEES TO HOME
ORGANIZATION: THE GODFATHER APPROACH
182   Noer, D.M., Personnel Journal, January 1974,
      pp. 45-51.

RE-ORIENTATION OF OVERSEAS WORKERS TO THEIR HOMELAND
183   Global Community Centre, Box One Million, 94
      Queen St., South Kitchener, Ontario N2G 1V9

SUCCESSFUL REPATRIATION DEMANDS ATTENTION, CARE AND
A DASH OF INGENUITY
184   Shabaz, W.O., Business International, March 3,
      1978.

THE HAZARDS OF COMING HOME
185   Smith, L., Dun's Review, October 1975, pp. 71-73.

THESE EXECUTIVES WON'T COME HOME
186   Dun's Review, November 1972.

G. *Personnel Departments and Policies*

PERSONNEL PRACTICES OF AMERICAN COMPANIES IN EUROPE, U.S.A.
187   Chruden, H.J. and Sherman, A.W. Jr., American Management Association, Inc., 1972.

A STUDY OF EMPLOYEE RELOCATION POLICIES AMONG MAJOR U.S. CORPORATIONS, 1980; RELOCATION MANAGEMENT '80 PROCEEDINGS
188   Merrill Lynch Relocation Management Inc., 4 Corporate Park Drive, White Plains, NY 10604.

THE PERSONNEL MANAGER FOR INTERNATIONAL OPERATIONS
189   Oxley, G.M., Personnel, Vol. 38, No. 6, November-December 1961, pp. 52-58.

MANAGEMENT DEVELOPMENT IN ETHNOCENTRIC MULTINATIONAL CORPORATIONS
190   Zeira, Y., California Management Review, Vol. 18, No. 4, Summer 1976, pp. 34-42.

OVERLOOKED PERSONNEL PROBLEMS OF MULTINATIONAL CORPORATIONS
191   Zeira, Y., Columbia Journal of World Business, Vol. 10, No. 2, Summer 1975, pp. 96-103.

THE ROLE OF THE TRAINING DIRECTOR IN MULTINATIONAL
CORPORATIONS

192 Zeira, Y., Training and Development Journal,
March 1979, p. 20.

H. *Measuring Performance*

MANAGEMENT ASSESSMENT IN INTERNATIONAL ORGANIZATIONS
193 Kraut, A.I., Industrial Relations, May 1973,
pp. 172-182.

MEASURING SUCCESSFUL PERFORMANCE OVERSEAS
194 Peter, H.W. and Henry, E.R., International
Development Review, Volume 3, No. 3, 1961,
pp. 8-12.

7
TRANSFER OF IDEAS

TESTING MANAGEMENT THEORIES CROSS-CULTURALLY
195 Bennett, M., Journal of Applied Psychology,
Vol. 62, No. 5, 1977, pp. 578-581.

IDENTIFICATION OF OPINION LEADERS ACROSS CULTURES:
AN ASSESSMENT FOR USE IN THE DIFFUSION OF INNOVATIONS
AND IDEAS
196 Cosmas, S.C. and Sheth, J.N., Journal of
International Business Studies, Spring-Summer
1980, pp. 66-72.

MOTIVATION, LEADERSHIP AND ORGANIZATION: DO AMERICAN
THEORIES APPLY ABROAD?
197 Hofstede, G., Organizational Dynamics, Summer
1980, pp. 42-64.

A MODEL FOR ANALYZING THE UNIVERSALITY AND TRANS-
FERABILITY OF MANAGEMENT
198 Koontz, H., Academy of Management Journal,
December 1969, pp. 415-429.

8
TRANSFER OF PRACTICES
(MANAGEMENT AND TRAINING)

THE APPLICABILITY OF AMERICAN MANAGEMENT PRACTICES
TO DEVELOPING COUNTRIES: A CASE STUDY OF THE
PHILIPPINES

199 Flores, F., Management International Review,
January 1972, pp. 83-90.

THE TRANSFER OF MANAGEMENT KNOW-HOW TO DEVELOPING
COUNTRIES

200 Kohler, K.G., Management International
Review, Vol. 6, 1971, pp. 122-124.

A RESEARCH MODEL TO DETERMINE THE APPLICABILITY OF
AMERICAN MANAGEMENT KNOW-HOW IN DIFFERING CULTURES
AND/OR ENVIRONMENT

201 Negandhi, A.R. and Estafen, B.D., Journal of
the Academy of Management, Volume 8, 1965,
pp. 309-318.

THE STUDY OF THE TRANSFER OF TRAINING FROM DEVELOPED
TO LESS DEVELOPED COUNTRIES: THE CASE OF CHINA

202 Sarpong, K. and Rawls, J.R., Journal of
Management Studies, Vol. XII, 1976, p. 16.

9
TRANSFER OF PRODUCTS
(MARKETING)

CAN YOU STANDARDIZE MULTINATIONAL MARKETING?
203 Buzzell, R.D., Harvard Business Review, Vol. 46, 1968, pp. 102-113.

PATTERNS OF MARKETING ADAPTATION IN INTERNATIONAL BUSINESS: A STUDY OF AMERICAN BUSINESS FIRMS OPERATING IN INDIA
204 Kacker, M.P., Management International Review, 1972, pp. 111-118.

10
STAFFING

MULTINATIONAL MANAGEMENT STAFFING WITH AMERICAN
EXPATRIATES
205 Baker, J.C. and Ivancevich, J.M., Economic and
Business Bulletin, Fall 1970, Vol. 23, No. 1,
pp. 35-40.

HOW TO BUILD AN EXCELLENT INTERNATIONAL STAFF
206 Beeth, G., International Management Practice,
AMACOM, a Division of American Management
Associations, 1973, pp. 66-81.

HOW GRUMMAN MANAGES EXPATRIATE STAFFING FOR MAJOR
IRANIAN PROJECT
207 Business International, December 3, 1976,
pp. 387-388.

SOURCES OF MANAGEMENT PROBLEMS IN JAPANESE-AMERICAN
JOINT VENTURES
208 Peterson, R.B. and Shimada, J.Y., Academy of
Management Review, Vol. 3, No. 4, October 1978,
pp. 796-805.

THE STAFFING OF FOREIGN DIVISIONS AND BRANCHES
209 Steinmetz, L.L., Unpublished Ph.D. dissertation,
Department of Economics, University of Michigan,
1964.

CONSIDERATIONS IN STAFFING FOR OVERSEAS MANAGEMENT
NEEDS

210   Voris, W.D., <u>Personnel Journal</u>, June 1975,
       pp. 332-333, 354.

GENUINE MULTINATIONAL STAFFING POLICY: EXPECTATIONS
AND REALITIES

211   Zeira, Y., <u>Academy of Management Journal</u>,
       Vol. 20, No. 2, June 1977, pp. 327-333.

11
FOREIGN NATIONALS OVERSEAS

CURRENT PATTERNS AND FUTURE TRENDS IN EMPLOYMENT,
AND TRAINING AND DEVELOPMENT PROGRAMS FOR FOREIGN
NATIONAL MANAGERS
212 Carr, N., Academy of Management Proceedings,
1972, pp. 336-339.

THE NON-AMERICAN MANAGER, ESPECIALLY AS THIRD COUNTRY
NATIONAL, IN U.S. MULTINATIONALS: A SEPARATE BUT
EQUAL DOCTRINE?
213 Daniels, J.D., Journal of International
Business Studies, Vol. 5, No. 2, Fall 1974,
pp. 25-41.

HOW TO MINIMIZE OVERSEAS RECRUITING RISKS
214 DeGenring, W.J., Management Review, March 1967,
pp. 12-18.

DEVELOPING EXECUTIVES FOR FOREIGN OPERATIONS: I -
TRAINING MANAGERS IN LATIN AMERICA - A SURVEY OF
COMPANY PRACTICE
215 Dickerman, A.B. and Davis, R.G., Personnel,
May-June 1966, pp. 57-61.

TRAINING MANAGERS ABROAD
216 Dustan, J. and Makanowitzky, B., The Council
for International Progress in Management,
(U.S.A.) Inc., 1960, 527 pp.

SUGGESTED CRITERIA FOR SELECTING MANAGEMENT
CONSULTANTS IN DEVELOPING COUNTRIES
217 Eldin, H.K. and Sadig, S., International
Management Review, 1971, pp. 123-132.

DEVELOPING OVERSEAS MANAGERS AND MANAGERS OVERSEAS
218 Illman, P.E., New York, NY: AMACOM, 1979.

DEVELOPING MANAGERS IN OVERSEAS OPERATIONS
219 Lee, J., Harvard Business Review, November-
December, 1968.

INCOMPETENT FOREIGN MANAGERS?
220 McKenzie, C., Business Horizons, Spring 1966,
pp. 83-90.

INCENTIVES FOR FOREIGN NATIONALS
221 Rock, M. and Sym-Smith, C.I., Harvard Business
Review, March-April 1973, pp. 33-42.

DEVELOPING EXECUTIVES FOR FOREIGN OPERATIONS II:
MANAGEMENT DEVELOPMENT IN OVERSEAS BRANCHES - ONE
COMPANY'S PROGRAM
222 Rodgers, C.R.P., Personnel, May-June 1966,
pp. 62-66.

UNDERSTAND YOUR OVERSEAS WORKFORCE
223 Sirota, D. and Greenwood, J.M., Harvard
Business Review, January-February 1971, pp. 53-
60.

HOST COUNTRY MANAGERS OF MULTINATIONAL FIRMS: AN
EVALUATION OF VARIABLES AFFECTING THEIR MANAGERIAL
THINKING PATTERNS
224 Toyne, B., Journal of International Business
Studies, Vol. 7, No. 2, Spring 1976, pp. 39-55.

THE MULTINATIONAL BUSINESS ORGANIZATION: A SCHEME FOR
THE TRAINING OF OVERSEAS PERSONNEL IN COMMUNICATION
225 Yousef, F.S. and Briggs, N.E., International
and Intercultural Communication Annual, Speech
Communication Association, Chicago, IL:
Intercultural Press, Inc., 1975, Vol. II,
pp. 74-85.

THE INTEGRATION OF LOCAL NATIONALS INTO THE MANAGERIAL
HIERARCHY OF AMERICAN OVERSEAS SUBSIDIARIES: AN
EXPLORATORY STUDY
226 Youssef, S.M., Academy of Management Journal,
Vol. 16, No. 1, March 1973, pp. 24-35.

MANAGING THIRD-COUNTRY NATIONALS IN MNC'S
227 Zeira, Y., Business Horizons, Vol. 20, No. 5,
October 1977, pp. 83-88.

OVERCOMING THE RESISTANCE OF MULTINATIONAL CORPORA-
TIONS TO ATTITUDE SURVEYS OF HOST-COUNTRY ORGANIZATIONS
228 Zeira, Y., Columbia Journal of World Business,
forthcoming.

THIRD-COUNTRY MANAGERS IN MULTINATIONAL CORPORATIONS
229 Zeira, Y., Personnel Review, Vol. 6, No. 1,
January 1977, pp. 32-37.

12
IMPACT OF CORPORATION
ON LOCAL CULTURE

THE MULTINATIONAL FIRM AND HOST ARAB SOCIETY: AREAS
OF CONFLICT AND CONVERGENCE
230 Ajami, R.A., Management International Review,
Vol. 20, No. 1, 1980, pp. 16-27.

TRANSNATIONAL CORPORATIONS: THEIR IMPACT ON THIRD
WORLD SOCIETIES AND CULTURES
231 Kumar, K., Honolulu, HI: Westview Press, 1980.

THE EFFECTS OF TRANSNATIONAL CORPORATIONS ON CULTURE
232 Sunkel, O. and Fuenzalida, E., Paris: UNESCO,
1976.

13
HOW FOREIGNERS SEE AMERICANS

EUROPEANS SAY: U.S. EXECUTIVES AREN'T SO GREAT
233   Dun's Review, January 1973, p. 51.

OUR EXPERIENCE WITH AN AMERICAN COMPANY
234   Matsumoto, H., Conference Board Record, April
       1972, pp. 35-37.

NOBODY LIKES TO WORK FOR AMERICANS
235   Zimmerer, C., Christian Science Monitor,
       December 12, 1978.

14
FOREIGN NATIONALS IN THE U.S.

ORGANIZATIONAL CHANGES OF A JAPANESE FIRM IN AMERICA
236 Amano, M.M., California Management Review, Vol. XXI, No. 3, Spring 1979, pp. 51-60.

MADE IN AMERICA (UNDER JAPANESE MANAGEMENT)
237 Johnson, R.T. and Ouchi, W.G., Harvard Business Review, Vol. 52, No. 5, September-October 1974, pp. 61-69.

THE UPROOTED EUROPEAN MANAGER IN AMERICA
238 Leontiades, J., European Business, Winter 1973.

EUROPEANS IN AMERICA PRACTICE 'FOREIGN' MANAGEMENT
239 Rohan, T.M., Industry Week, January 22, 1979.

15
LEARNING FROM
FOREIGN NATIONALS

WHAT WE CAN LEARN FROM JAPANESE MANAGEMENT
240   Drucker, P.F., The McKinsey Quarterly, Winter 1973.

LEARNING FROM FOREIGN MANAGEMENT
241   Drucker, P.F., Wall Street Journal, June 4, 1980.

LEARNING FROM THE JAPANESE: WHAT OR HOW?
242   Marengo, F., Management International Review, Vol. 19, No. 4, 1979, pp. 39-47.

JAPANESE PARTICIPATIVE MANAGEMENT, OR HOW THE RINGI SEIDO CAN WORK FOR YOU
243   Moran, R.T., Advanced Management Journal, Summer 1979, pp. 14-22.

THEORY Z HOW AMERICAN BUSINESS CAN MEET THE JAPANESE CHALLENGE
244   Ouchi, W., Addison-Wesley Publishing, Inc., 1981

ZEN AND THE ART OF MANAGEMENT
245   Pascale, R.T., Harvard Business Review, March-April 1978, pp. 153-162.

48

THE ART OF JAPANESE MANAGEMENT: APPLICATIONS FOR
AMERICAN EXECUTIVES
246   Pascale, R.T. and Athos, A.G., New York, NY:
       Simon & Shuster, 1981.

JAPAN AS NUMBER ONE: LESSONS FOR AMERICA
247   Vogel, E.F., New York, NY: Harper and Row, 1979

16
RELATIONS WITH
NATIONALS FROM SPECIFIC COUNTRIES

A.   INFORMATION ON NUMEROUS COUNTRIES

COMMUNICATION LEARING AIDS

248   B.Y.U. Center for International and Area Studies, Publications Services, 130 F.O.B., Provo, Utah 84602. Booklets currently available ($2.00 each) include the following:

People of Brazil
French-Speaking People
   of Europe
German-Speaking People
   of Europe
People of Hong Kong
People of Japan

Latin Americans
People of the
   Philippines
Samoans
People of Spain
People of Thailand

CULTURGRAMS

249   B.Y.U. Center for International and Area
Studies, Publications Services, 130 F.O.B.,
Provo, Utah 84602. 4 pp. each. 25¢ each.
Available for the following countries:

Argentina	Japan
Australia	Korea
Austria	Lebanon
Belgium (Flemish)	Luxembourg
Belgium (French)	Malaysia
Bolivia	Mexico
Brazil	Netherlands
Bulgaria	New Zealand
Canada (Eastern)	Nicaragua
Canada (French)	Nigeria
Canada (Western)	Norway
Chile	Okinawa
China	Pakistan
Columbia	Panama
Costa Rica	Paraguay
Denmark	Peru
Ecuador	Philippines
Egypt	Poland
El Salvador	Portugal
England	Puerto Rico
Fiji	Samoa
Finland	Saudi Arabia
France	Scotland
Germany	Singapore
Ghana	South Africa
Greece	Spain
Guatemala	Sri Lanka
Honduras	Sweden
Hong Kong	Switzerland
Iceland	Tahiti
India	Republic of China
Indonesia	(Taiwan)
Iran	Thailand
Republic of Ireland	Tonga
Ireland (Northern)	Uruguay
Israel (Jewish)	USSR
Israel (Palestine Arab)	Venezuela
Italy	Wales

CULTURAL SPECIFICS FOR MANAGEMENT EFFECTIVENESS

250 Harris, P.R. and Moran, R.T., Managing Cultural Differences, Unit 4, Houston, TX: Gulf Publishing Co., 1979, pp. 212-347. Countries covered include: England, Ireland, Japan, People's Republic of China, Saudi Arabia, Iran.

UPDATES

251 Lanier, A.R., Chicago, IL: Intercultural Press, Inc. Volumes now available on the following countries:

Bahrain/Qatar	Kuwait
Belgium	Mexico
Brazil	Nigeria
Britain	Saudi Arabia
Egypt	Singapore
France	South Korea
Hong Kong	R.O.C. (Taiwan)
Indonesia	Venezuela
Japan	West Germany
	United Arab Emirates

INTERACTS: INTERCULTURAL RELATIONS IN BUSINESS

252 Renwick, G.W., Chicago, IL: Intercultural Press, Inc. Volumes now available or in preparation are:

Australia - U.S., Renwick, G.W.
Mexico - U.S., Condon, J.C.
Thailand - U.S., Fieg, J.P.
French and English in Canada, Hawes, F.
Japan - U.S., Condon, J.C.
Malaysia - U.S., Renwick, G.W.

B. REGIONS

THE MULTINATIONAL FIRM AND HOST ARAB SOCIETY: AREAS
OF CONFLICT AND CONVERGENCE
253 Ajami, R.A., Management International Review,
Vol. 20, No. 1, 1980, pp. 16-27.

PERSONNEL PRACTICES OF AMERICAN COMPANIES IN EUROPE
254 Chruden, H.J. and Sherman, A.W., Jr., U.S.A.:
American Management Association, Inc., 1972.

U.S. VS. LATIN-AMERICA: BUSINESS AND CULTURE
255 Davis, S.M., Harvard Business Review, November-
December 1969.

DEVELOPING EXECUTIVES FOR FOREIGN OPERATIONS: I -
TRAINING MANAGERS IN LATIN AMERICA - A SURVEY OF
COMPANY PRACTICE
256 Dickerman, A.B. and Davis, R.G., Personnel,
May-June 1966, pp. 57-61.

A GUIDE TO DOING BUSINESS ON THE ARABIAN PENINSULA
257 Fleming, Q.W., New York, NY: AMACOM, 1981.

LEADERSHIP ATTITUDES OF AMERICAN AND GERMAN EXPATRIATE
MANAGERS IN EUROPE AND LATIN AMERICA
258 Miller, E., Bhatt, B., Hill, R. and Catteaneo,
J., Academy of Management Proceedings, Vol. 40,
1980, pp. 53-57.

CULTURAL SPECIFICS AND SYNERGY

259 Moran, R.T. and Harris, P.R., <u>Managing Cultural Synergy</u>, Unit Three, Houston, TX: Gulf Publishing Co., 1981. Regions covered are: Asia, Middle East, Europe and Latin America.

A PRACTICAL GUIDE TO LIVING AND TRAVEL IN THE ARAB WORLD

260 Shilling, N.A., New York, NY: Inter-Crescent Publishing & Information Corp., 1978.

DOING BUSINESS WITH LATIN NATIONALISTS

261 Utley, J.B., <u>Harvard Business Review</u>, January-February 1973, pp. 77-87.

HOST COUNTRY ORGANIZATIONS AND EXPATRIATE MANAGERS IN EUROPE

262 Zeira, Y. and Harrari, E., <u>California Management Review</u>, Vol. 21, No. 3, Spring 1979, pp. 40-50.

C. SPECIFIC COUNTRIES

Canada

HOW THE JAPANESE ARE MANAGING IN CANADA
263   Morgan, K., Executive, March 1974, pp. 39-42.

China

DOING BUSINESS IN THE PEOPLE'S REPUBLIC OF CHINA
264   Moran, R.T. and Hall, D., Audio Cassette and
       Manual, Chicago, IL: Intercultural Press, Inc.,
       1981.

EAST MEETS WEST: CHINA FOR AMERICAN MANAGERS
265   Tsurumi, Y., Columbia Journal of World Business,
       Issue 1, Winter 1977, p. 59.

Costa Rica

U.S. MNC-HOST GOVERNMENT JOINT VENTURES IN COSTA RICA:
A COMPARATIVE ANALYSIS OF THE ATTITUDES OF U.S. MNCs
AND OF HOST COUNTRY EXECUTIVES
266   Raveed, S., Academy of Management Proceedings,
       1977, pp. 327-332.

France

HOW TO DO BUSINESS WITH A FRENCHMAN
267   Eggers, E.R., Harper's Magazine, August 1965,
       pp. 41-44.

Germany

MEETING GERMAN BUSINESS: A PRACTICAL GUIDE FOR
AMERICAN AND OTHER ENGLISH-SPEAKING BUSINESSMEN IN
GERMANY
268 Burmeister, I., Hamburg, Germany: Atlantik-
Brucke, 1977.

COMMUNICATION BARRIERS BETWEEN GERMAN SUBSIDIARIES
AND PARENT AMERICAN COMPANIES
269 Hildebrandt, H.W., Michigan Business Review,
July 1973.

India

APPLYING NEW KNOWLEDGE IN THE BACK-HOME SETTING: A
STUDY OF INDIAN MANAGERS' ADOPTIVE EFFORTS
270 Baumgartel, H. and Jeanpierre, F., Journal
of Applied Behavioural Science, Vol. 8, No. 6,
November-December 1972, pp. 674-695.

PATTERNS OF MARKETING ADAPTATION IN INTERNATIONAL
BUSINESS: A STUDY OF AMERICAN BUSINESS FIRMS OPERATING
IN INDIA
271 Kacker, M.P., Management International Review,
Vol. 4, No. 5, 1972, pp. 111-118.

Iran

HOW GRUMMAN MANAGES EXPATRIATE STAFFING FOR MAJOR
IRANIAN PROJECT
272 Business International, December 3, 1976,
pp. 387-388.

Japan

JOINT VENTURES IN JAPAN AND HOW TO OBTAIN MANAGERIAL
CONTROL
273 Baker, J.C. and Kondo, T., M.S.U. Business
Topics, Vol. 19, No. 1, Winter 1971, pp. 48-54.

TRAINING EXPATRIATES FOR MANAGERIAL ASSIGNMENT IN
JAPAN
274 Harrari, E. and Zeira, Y., California
Management Review, Vol. 20, No. 4, Summer 1978,
pp. 56-62.

A COMPARATIVE STUDY OF PERSONNEL PROBLEMS IN INTER-
NATIONAL COMPANIES AND JOINT VENTURES IN JAPAN
275 Peterson, R.B. and Schwind, H.F., Journal of
International Business Studies, Vol. 8, No. 1,
Spring-Summer 1977, pp. 45-57.

PERSONNEL PROBLEMS IN INTERNATIONAL COMPANIES AND
JOINT VENTURES IN JAPAN
276 Peterson, R.B. and Schwind, H.F., Academy of
Management Proceedings, Vol. 35, 1975, pp. 282-284.

SOURCES OF MANAGEMENT PROBLEMS IN JAPANESE-AMERICAN
JOINT VENTURES
277 Peterson, R.B. and Shimada, J.Y., Academy of
Management Review, Vol. 3, No. 4, October 1978,
pp. 796-805.

MYTHS THAT MISLEAD U.S. MANAGERS IN JAPAN
278 Tsurumi, Y., Harvard Business Review, July-
August 1971, pp. 118-128.

TRAINING OF EXPATRIATES FOR MANAGERIAL ASSIGNMENTS IN
JAPAN
279 Zeira, Y. and Harrari, E., California Management
Review, Vol. 20, No. 4, Summer 1978.

17
BASIC SOURCES ON
INTERCULTURAL COMMUNICATION

HANDBOOK OF INTERCULTURAL COMMUNICATION
280 Asante, M.K., Newmark, E. and Blake, C.A.,
     Beverly Hills, CA: Sage Publications, 1979.

CULTURES IN CONTACT: STUDIES IN CROSS-CULTURAL
INTERACTIONS
281 Bochner, S., New York, NY: Pergamon Press,
     1981.

INTERCULTURAL COMMUNICATING
282 B.Y.U. Center for International and Area
     Studies, Publications Services, 130 F.O.B.,
     Provo, Utah 84602.

THE INTERNATIONAL FAMILY
283 B.Y.U. Center for International and Area
     Studies, Publications Services, 130 F.O.B.,
     Provo, Utah 84602.

JET LAG AND DECISION-MAKING
284 B.Y.U. Center for International and Area
     Studies, Publications Services, 130 F.O.B.,
     Provo, Utah 84602.

CROSS-CULTURAL ENCOUNTERS: FACE-TO-FACE INTERACTION
285 Brislin, R.W., New York, NY: Pergamon Press,
     1981.

CROSS-CULTURAL ORIENTATION PROGRAMS
286 Brislin, R.W. and Pedersen, P.B., New York, NY: Gardner Press, Inc., 1976.

INTERCULTURAL AND INTERNATIONAL COMMUNICATIONS
287 Casmir, F.L. (ed.), Washington, DC: University Press of America, 1978.

TRAINING FOR THE CROSS-CULTURAL MIND
288 Casse, P., Washington, DC: The Society for Intercultural Education, Training and Research, 1980.

AN INTRODUCTION TO INTERCULTURAL COMMUNICATION
289 Condon, J.C. and Yousef, F., Indianapolis, IN: Bobbs-Merrill, 1975.

INTERNATIONAL AND INTERCULTURAL COMMUNICATION
290 Fischer, H.D. and Merrill, J.C., New York, NY: Hastings House, 1980.

AN ANALYSIS OF HUMAN RELATIONS TRAINING AND ITS IMPLICATIONS FOR OVERSEAS PERFORMANCE
291 Foster, R.J. and Danielian, J., Alexandria, VA: Human Resources Research Office, 1966.

BEYOND CULTURE
292 Hall, E.T., Garden City, NY: Anchor Books, 1979.

THE SILENT LANGUAGE
293 Hall, E.T., Greenwich, CT: Fawcett Publications, Inc., 1959.

CANADIANS IN DEVELOPMENT: AN EMPIRICAL STUDY OF ADJUSTMENT AND EFFECTIVENESS ON OVERSEAS ASSIGNMENTS
294 Hawes, F. and Kealy, D., Ottawa, Canada: Communications Branch, Briefing Center, Canadian International Development, Agency, 1979.

INTERCULTURAL SOURCEBOOK: CROSS-CULTURAL TRAINING METHODOLOGIES
295 Hoopes, D.S and Ventura, P., Chicago, IL: Intercultural Press, Inc., 1979

INTERNATIONAL JOURNAL OF INTERCULTURAL RELATIONS
296   Landis, D. (ed.), New York, NY: Pergamon Press, Quarterly.

EVALUATION HANDBOOK FOR CROSS-CULTURAL TRAINING
297   Renwick, G.W., Chicago, IL: Intercultural Press, Inc., 1980.

ASSESSING COMMUNICATION COMPETENCY FOR INTERCULTURAL ADAPTATION
298   Ruben, B.D., Group and Organization Studies, Vol. 1, No. 3, September 1976, pp. 334-354.

INTERCULTURAL COMMUNICATION: A READER
299   Samovar, L.A. and Porter, R.E., Second Edition, Belmont, CA: Wadsworth Publishing Co., 1976.

UNDERSTANDING INTERCULTURAL COMMUNICATION
300   Samovar, L.A., Porter, R.E. and Jain, N.C., Belmont, CA: Wadsworth Publishing Co., 1981.

TOWARDS INTERNATIONALISM: READINGS IN CROSS-CULTURAL COMMUNICATIONS
301   Smith, E.C. and Luce, L.B. (eds.), Rowley, MA: Newbury House, 1979.

INTERNATIONAL AND INTERCULTURAL COMMUNICATION ANNUAL
302   Speech Communication Association, Chicago, IL: Intercultural Press, Inc., 1974 to Present.

AMERICAN CULTURAL PATTERNS
303   Stewart, E.C., Chicago, IL: Intercultural Press, Inc., 1971.

INDEX OF AUTHORS

INDEX OF JOURNALS